Original title:
The Echoes of Empathy

Copyright © 2024 Swan Charm
All rights reserved.

Editor: 978-9916-86-558-3
Author: Sara Säde
ISBN HARDBACK: 978-9916-86-557-6
ISBN PAPERBACK: 978-9916-86-558-3
ISBN EBOOK: 978-9916-86-559-0

The Strength of Gentle Hands

Gentle hands hold the weight,
Softly grasping dreams anew.
With each touch, love emanates,
Building bridges, firm and true.

In quiet moments, hearts entwine,
Strength found in a tender grace.
In this dance, we intertwine,
Finding solace in embrace.

Hands that heal, hands that guide,
In the shadows, they bring light.
With every whisper, hope applied,
Transforming darkness into bright.

Let them cradle, let them lace,
Through storms and calm, they thrive.
In the warmth of their embrace,
Together, we will survive.

So take my hand, let's gently hold,
In this journey, side by side.
Through every story yet untold,
Our strength in love, our guide.

Unfolding Together

Like petals bloom in springtime sun,
Two hearts begin to intertwine.
In laughter shared, a journey's spun,
Moments cherished, soft as wine.

With every step, we share the air,
Two souls weaving threads of fate.
In corners bright, we leave our care,
Together, we create and wait.

Fates aligned, a tapestry,
Each thread held firm in passion's thread.
In whispered dreams, we set them free,
In every loss, new paths are spread.

Through every storm, we find a way,
With gentle smiles and hands held tight.
We'll face the night, we'll chase the day,
Unfolding, two in shared delight.

In this dance, no end in sight,
Boundless love in every weather.
Here we are, hearts shining bright,
Together blessed, forever tethered.

The Subtle Art of Bearing Witness

In silent corners, shadows play,
Awareness blooms in quiet tides.
With every breath, we find our way,
To hold the truth where love abides.

Eyes that listen, hearts that see,
In the smallest act, we find grace.
Bearing witness, we choose to be,
A sanctuary, a safe space.

Moments fleeting, yet profound,
With gentle smiles, we hold the space.
In every story that we've found,
Compassion flows, our warm embrace.

Unspoken words in shared delight,
We lean into the weight of pain.
In understanding, we ignite,
The bright, enduring hope we gain.

Through darkened paths, we walk as one,
Holding stories, dreams laid bare.
In every battle, love is spun,
The subtle art, our hearts declare.

In the Heart's Embrace

In the heart's embrace, we reside,
Where whispers echo soft and true.
Each secret shared, our souls confide,
United here, just me and you.

Canvas painted with our dreams,
Strokes of laughter, tears combined.
In the quiet, love redeems,
With every memory, we've aligned.

Through winding paths, we seek the light,
In shadows cast, we find our way.
With open hearts, we face the night,
In every dawn, a brand new day.

So let us soar on wings of trust,
In every moment, love's sweet grace.
Together forged, in hope we must,
Embrace the world, our sacred space.

For in this bond, we plant our seeds,
Of kindness, joy, and endless care.
In the heart's embrace, love leads,
A journey rich, beyond compare.

The Texture of Togetherness

In the woven threads of life,
We find each other's hands.
A tapestry of laughter,
And quiet, understanding strands.

When storms of doubt surround us,
We shelter close and warm.
Together we are stronger,
United in every form.

In silence, we create space,
For comfort to unfold.
Two hearts beat in rhythm,
In a language never told.

Through seasons' ebb and flow,
We cherish every grace.
The texture of togetherness,
In every shared embrace.

With every joy and sorrow,
A bond begins to grow.
The fabric of our journey,
Is stitched with threads of hope.

Responding to the Silence

In shadows where words falter,
We search for gentle signs.
A look, a soft acknowledgment,
In silence, love defines.

Each breath becomes a whisper,
A bridge across the void.
We listen to the echoes,
Of feelings once denied.

In moments bathed in quiet,
The heart begins to speak.
With patience, understanding,
We seek what words can't reach.

The stillness holds a message,
In every pause, a clue.
Responding to the silence,
I find my way to you.

Together in the quiet,
We learn to navigate.
These spaces filled with meaning,
Unfold as love's dictate.

In the Lull Between Words

Amidst the rush of conversations,
There's beauty in the pause.
In the lull between our words,
Our hearts begin to cause.

A moment where we linger,
In thoughts we cannot say.
Connections weave like music,
In silence, we portray.

Eyes speak in hushed volumes,
While fingers softly trace.
In the lull between our words,
We find a sacred space.

A sanctuary of feelings,
Where vulnerability reigns.
In these gentle interruptions,
Our deeper truth remains.

So let the silence breathe,
Let it cradle us anew.
In the lull between our words,
Our souls begin to view.

The Weight of Shared Grief

Underneath the heavy silence,
We carry burdens near.
The weight of shared grief,
A testament to tear.

In hushed tones, we gather,
To honor what we've lost.
Every memory a treasure,
But at a heavy cost.

Yet in this shared lament,
A bond begins to form.
We find strength in our sorrow,
And beauty in the storm.

With every cry and tremor,
The heart learns to release.
The weight of shared grief lightens,
In empathy, we find peace.

Together in our aching,
We weave a tender thread.
The weight of shared grief shared,
Is a path that we have tread.

Bridges of Warmth

Across the shimmering stream,
We build our towers tall and bright.
With gentle hands and hopeful dreams,
We light the shadows in the night.

The sun sets soft upon our backs,
As laughter dances in the breeze.
Together on the winding tracks,
Our hearts find strength and find their ease.

With every step, our voices blend,
Creating music in the air.
With every bridge, our souls transcend,
A tapestry of love and care.

Though storms may come, we will stand strong,
Bound by the warmth, our spirits soar.
Together, we will sing our song,
And forge a path forevermore.

Each bridge we build holds stories shared,
Of journeys long and futures bright.
Together, always, hearts laid bare,
We'll conquer darkness with our light.

Tapestries of Sorrow and Solace

In shadows deep, we weave our thread,
Each stitch a tale of pain and grace.
The colors blend where once we bled,
Creating beauty in this space.

With every knot, a memory tied,
The fabric holds our whispered fears.
But in the darkness, hope's our guide,
Embracing joy amidst the tears.

Through woven paths, we find our way,
A delicate dance of loss and gain.
In tangled threads, our spirits play,
Emerging stronger from the pain.

The tapestry, both worn and wise,
Reflects the struggles we have faced.
In every tear, a new sunrise,
In sorrow's grip, we find our place.

With hands entwined, we stand as one,
In unity, our voices rise.
From sorrow's depths, our hearts have spun,
A tapestry beneath the skies.

Seeds of Nurtured Hope

In tiny hands, we hold the earth,
The promise life begins to bloom.
With heartfelt care, we plant our worth,
And watch creation chase the gloom.

Each seed a story waiting long,
To break the soil and reach for light.
With patience, we will grow so strong,
In whispers shared, our dreams take flight.

Through seasons shifting, roots will spread,
As laughter mingles with the rain.
In every challenge, courage bred,
Our hopes emerge from gentle pain.

We'll nurture love and watch it thrive,
With kindness lending strength and grace.
Together, we will come alive,
Our garden blooms, a warm embrace.

With every dawn, new life appears,
A testament of all we've sown.
In fields of gold, through laughter, tears,
Our seeds of hope have found a home.

Garden of Empathetic Hearts

In quiet corners, souls entwine,
Where understanding gently grows.
With every word, a thread so fine,
In this garden, love bestows.

Soft petals whisper tales of trust,
As hearts unfold, revealing light.
Together in this bond, we must,
Unravel darkness, share the fight.

We nurture kindness, sowing care,
In sacred soil, our truths arise.
Each moment shared, a breath we share,
In empathy where hope defies.

With every breeze that stirs the leaves,
We listen close to hearts in need.
Through shared compassion, our soul weaves,
A tapestry of love's great deed.

In this garden, shade and sun,
We gather strength to face the storm.
In empathetic hearts, we run,
Together, keeping love so warm.

Whispers of Understanding

In the still of the night, secrets weave,
Gentle voices, softly they grieve.
Through the shadows, truths unfold,
In whispered tales, bright and bold.

Hearts beat softly, rhythms align,
In hidden corners, sparkles shine.
A knowing glance, a shared sigh,
Together we stand, you and I.

Under the stars, we find our way,
Navigating dreams, come what may.
In quiet moments, we create the space,
For love to flourish in tender grace.

With every word, a bridge is built,
In the tapestry of trust, no guilt.
Embracing shadows, we find the light,
Together we journey, through the night.

In the dance of souls, we intertwine,
With every heartbeat, your heart next to mine.
In whispers soft, our truths ignite,
A love resplendent, forever bright.

Tides of Connection

Like the waves that kiss the shore,
Our spirits meet, we crave for more.
The ebb and flow, a sacred dance,
In every glance, a second chance.

Underneath the moon's soft glow,
We navigate, together, slow.
Through currents deep, our hearts align,
In the ocean of souls, forever entwined.

Each ripple carries dreams untold,
In waves of laughter, brave and bold.
With open hearts, we ride the tide,
In this sea of love, we shall abide.

As the waters rise and fall anew,
Our connection grows, ever true.
In every storm, we stand as one,
Together we shine, like the sun.

Through the tides of life, we journey far,
Guided by love, our shining star.
In every moment, we find our way,
In the dance of the tides, we choose to stay.

Silence Between Heartbeats

In the quiet spaces, peace resides,
Between each heartbeat, love abides.
A gentle pause, a moment's grace,
In silence, we find our sacred place.

With every breath, the world slows down,
In stillness, joy wears a golden crown.
Eyes meet softly, words go unspoken,
In the quiet, hearts beat, unbroken.

A shared existence, no need for sound,
In whispered moments, love is found.
In the hush of night, we dream as one,
Under the gaze of the silent sun.

Every heartbeat a promise made,
In the silence, foundations laid.
Holding each other, in the embrace,
Finding solace in this sacred space.

Life unfolds in each tender pause,
In the rhythm of love, we find our cause.
In silence, we weave our perfect art,
Bound together, soul to heart.

Shadows of Compassion

In the twilight's glow, shadows play,
Compassion's light leads the way.
Through the dark, we walk with grace,
In every heart, a sacred place.

Underneath the stars so bright,
We share our fears, we share our light.
With gentle hands, we lift the fall,
In shadows deep, we hear the call.

Understanding blooms in quiet nights,
In the darkest corners, love ignites.
With every tear, a story shared,
In silent struggles, we are bared.

Together we rise, through pain and strife,
In the shadows, we celebrate life.
Compassion's embrace, a tender balm,
In each other's hearts, we find our calm.

In the dance of shadows, we find our way,
Through sorrow's depths, we learn to stay.
In every heartbeat, kindred souls,
Compassion weaves, and love consoles.

A Tapestry of Heartbeats

Threads of love weave softly,
In the loom of our days.
Each pulse calls out gently,
A rhythm that stays.

Whispers in the twilight,
Echoes of our dreams.
Together we create,
A symphony of beams.

Colors of our laughter,
Stitch together the past.
Patterns of our stories,
In memories cast.

Hearts entwined in silence,
With every shared glance.
A dance through the seasons,
In love's steady trance.

Every moment cherished,
In this fabric we spin.
A tapestry of heartbeats,
Where we both begin.

In the Wake of Kindness

Gentle gestures ripple,
Like waves upon the shore.
In the wake of kindness,
Hearts open, wanting more.

A smile shared over coffee,
A hand when we fall down.
Each act a small beacon,
Spreading joy around town.

Simple words exchanged,
In the morning light.
They soften the shadows,
And brighten the night.

Together we can mend,
The fractures in our souls.
In the wake of kindness,
We become more whole.

With every tiny action,
A ripple takes its flight.
Creating waves of goodness,
In the stillness of night.

The Language of Tenderness

In the hush of a moment,
Words float like soft clouds.
The language of tenderness,
That whispers in crowds.

Eyes that speak in silence,
A touch that tells so much.
Beneath all the chaos,
It's the gentle that will clutch.

Every heartbeat listens,
To the sighs that we share.
In the warmth of kindness,
Love's language, laid bare.

A soft breeze of comfort,
In the midst of the storm.
It cradles our worries,
Keeping us safe and warm.

In the tender exchanges,
We find our place to stand.
With the language of tenderness,
Together, hand in hand.

Intertwined Lives

In the fabric of time,
Our paths gently cross.
Intertwined lives linger,
No moment is lost.

Each story unfurling,
Like petals of a rose.
We write our own chapter,
In the way that it grows.

Memories like golden threads,
Stitched into our hearts.
In the quilt of existence,
Every piece plays its part.

With laughter as a mantra,
And tears as a guide.
Together, we flourish,
In the ebb and the tide.

Through seasons we wander,
In the dance of the fates.
Intertwined lives flourishing,
As love celebrates.

Ballads of Tenderness

In the soft glow of the evening light,
Whispers dance as dreams take flight.
Hearts entwined with gentle grace,
Finding warmth in a sweet embrace.

Through laughter shared and silent tears,
We weave our hopes, allaying fears.
Moments captured, pure and bright,
Echoing softly in the still of night.

Hands held tightly, our spirits soar,
Writing tales of love to explore.
Amid the chaos, we create our song,
In the tender spaces where we belong.

Every heartbeat a melody played,
In the symphony of trust displayed.
With each note that softly hums,
The ballads of tenderness become.

So let our voices rise and twine,
In a chorus of hearts that intertwine.
For in the quiet, our truth we find,
In endless rhythms, love unconfined.

Labyrinths of Shared Feelings

In the maze of thoughts we tread,
Winding pathways where silence led.
Each corner turned, emotions flow,
In shared secrets, our souls glow.

With whispers soft, we navigate,
Moments of doubt, we dissipate.
Holding hands through twists and bends,
Finding light where darkness ends.

The echoes of laughter, shadows blend,
In this labyrinth where hearts mend.
Together we travel, unafraid to roam,
In this shared space, we find our home.

Through questions asked and answers sought,
In the tapestry of care, we're caught.
Every thread, a story told,
In labyrinths of feelings, we behold.

So let us wander as one, entwined,
In this maze of hearts combined.
For every twist brings us near,
In the beauty of love, unshakable, clear.

Vibrations of Quiet Understanding

In the stillness where spirits meet,
There lies a rhythm, soft and sweet.
With each glance, a wordless bond,
Painting colors of love beyond.

In gentle nods and silent smiles,
We bridge the gaps that span the miles.
No need for words, the heart knows best,
In vibrations of calm, we find our rest.

Through the ebb and flow of shared sighs,
Understanding blooms without disguise.
In the quiet, our souls align,
In every heartbeat, your truth is mine.

With whispered thoughts, our spirits dance,
In the still of night, we find our chance.
To dive beneath the surface sheen,
In the vibrations, our love convenes.

So let the silence softly speak,
In the moments we cherish, not bleak.
For in quietude, we find our way,
In vibrations that linger, come what may.

Journeys of Kindred Hearts

With every step, we share the road,
In journeys where affection flowed.
Side by side through shadow and light,
Kindred hearts take flight in the night.

Across the miles, we trace our dreams,
In laughter's echo, love redeems.
Through tempests fierce and breezes mild,
The bond we share, forever wild.

In spoken words or simple signs,
We find the path where love aligns.
With open hearts, no fear of fate,
Together we traverse, never late.

Each moment captured, deeply sown,
In every journey, we have grown.
Through winding roads, we shall not part,
For this voyage is our tender art.

So let us wander, hand in hand,
In distant lands or desert sand.
For in the journey, the heart imparts,
The endless beauty of kindred hearts.

The Map of Our Vulnerability

In the silence, hearts lay bare,
Written paths of deep despair.
Each scar a marker, every tear,
A testament of what we fear.

With tender strokes, we trace the lines,
Finding comfort where love shines.
A fragile map, yet so defined,
In every fold, the truth we find.

Through whispered doubts and soft regrets,
We navigate the deep offsets.
Our souls exposed, yet standing strong,
In this journey, we belong.

Layers peeled back, revealing light,
Guiding us through darkest night.
Each moment shared, a gentle guide,
In vulnerability, we confide.

Conversations Without Sound

Eyes meet in a quiet dance,
Words unspoken, lost in chance.
Silent echoes fill the air,
In the stillness, feelings bare.

A smile exchanged, we understand,
Holding close, a tender hand.
Thoughts collide with every glance,
In this hush, we find romance.

Unvoiced dreams paint the night,
Inadequate words, yet hearts take flight.
Whispers linger deep inside,
Chasing shadows, we confide.

Moments stretch, time stands still,
In silence, we find our will.
Conversations that go unheard,
Speak the truth without a word.

Mirrored Emotions

Reflections dance on glassy seas,
Two souls caught in a gentle breeze.
What you feel, I too can sense,
In this bond, there's no pretense.

Mirrored gazes share a spark,
Illuminating spaces dark.
Emotions echo, rise and fall,
In this silence, we hear the call.

Love's embrace can shift like tide,
In mirrored waves, our truths collide.
With every shift, we learn and grow,
In each other, we see the flow.

Chasing feelings through the night,
In our hearts, we find the light.
Mirrored emotions, pure and free,
In this dance, it's you and me.

Beneath the Layers of Existence

Hidden worlds beneath our skin,
Stories waiting to begin.
Layers thick with joy and strife,
Each unveiling a part of life.

We peel away the masks we wear,
Searching deep, finding rare air.
In the depths, we find our truths,
Echoes of our shared youth.

Beyond the surface, we discover,
Timeless bonds that make us hover.
In between, the secrets seep,
Awakened dreams that never sleep.

Beneath the layers, hearts ignite,
Bursting forth with pure delight.
In this journey, hand in hand,
We unveil a wondrous land.

Catalysts for Gentle Change

In whispers soft, the breezes sway,
A spark ignites the break of day.
With kindness spread like morning light,
We turn the dark to purest bright.

Small gestures bloom like flowers fair,
A touch, a smile, a tender care.
Together we can shift the tide,
In gentle ways, our hearts abide.

As seasons change and time will flow,
The seeds we plant begin to grow.
In every heart, a flame can spark,
To guide the lost through shadows dark.

Like rivers winding through the land,
Our progress forged by every hand.
From little acts, a ripple spreads,
Creating paths where hope now leads.

So let us be the change we seek,
With open hearts, we grow and speak.
In unity, let's make our stand,
Catalysts for change, hand in hand.

Tides of Generosity

The ocean breathes with rhythmic grace,
As waves of kindness fill our space.
Each drop a token, pure and sweet,
A world transformed by love's heartbeat.

In moments shared and laughter bright,
We lift each other toward the light.
With open arms, we welcome all,
To stand as one, united, tall.

A simple gift can shift a fate,
With every course, we celebrate.
The tides of generosity, they swell,
In every heart, a story to tell.

Together we create the flow,
In giving, we begin to grow.
With selfless acts, we cast our nets,
And reap the joy that love begets.

So let us ride these waves of grace,
And share the wealth of every place.
In unity, our spirits soar,
The tides of love forever more.

Alchemy of Compassion

In the heart's forge where kindness glows,
The alchemist in each one knows.
Through acts of love, we blend and mend,
Transforming lives, our hearts extend.

With patience wrought from care and grace,
We find the light in every face.
In trials faced, we learn to bend,
Our brokenness a path to mend.

Each gentle word, a healing balm,
In chaos, we can find our calm.
Compassion's touch, a sacred art,
Can turn the tide, can heal the heart.

Through every struggle, we can rise,
With open hearts, we touch the skies.
No distance great, no bridge too wide,
When compassion flows, we stand beside.

In unity, we forge the way,
With empathy, we light the day.
The alchemy of love we've found,
Transforms our world, forever bound.

Murmurs of Intertwined Lives

In every story, threads are spun,
Lives intertwined, we're never done.
Through laughter shared and sorrows known,
A tapestry of love has grown.

Each moment lived, a stitch in time,
We weave our paths with love's pure rhyme.
In gentle bonds, our spirits soar,
Together find what we adore.

With open hearts, we share the load,
On winding paths, our journey flowed.
Through trials faced, connections deep,
In every soul, affection keeps.

With whispers soft, we call the past,
In memories shared, we find the vast.
Intertwined lives, a sacred dance,
In every glance, a touch, a chance.

So let us weave with threads of gold,
In unity, our hearts unfold.
For in this life, we thrive and grow,
In murmurs sweet, our love will show.

Hues of Compassionate Minds

In shades of blue, we find our calm,
A gentle touch, a soothing balm.
With every glance, a story shared,
In silent whispers, hearts are bared.

The canvas stretches, vibrant hues,
We paint our truths, we choose our views.
Through every tear, a rainbow born,
In unity, we rise reborn.

A palette rich with kindness spurred,
In every heart, compassion stirred.
Together we weave, no strand unwinds,
The art of love, in ink that binds.

From deepest red to the lightest white,
We learn to hold, to share the light.
In every stroke, a bond we find,
The hues of hearts, so intertwined.

Threads of Mutual Healing

In quiet moments, we reach out,
Thread by thread, dispel the doubt.
With every knot, a memory sewn,
Together, we mend what was once alone.

A tapestry of hopes entwined,
In every pull, compassion unconfined.
The wounds we share, they start to fade,
As threads of love and trust cascade.

With gentle hands, we weave our fate,
In every bond, we celebrate.
Each thread a promise, each stitch a care,
In healing fabric, we become aware.

The pattern shifts, the colors flow,
Through every challenge, we help each grow.
In unity, our strength revealed,
The threads of mutual healing sealed.

Lighthouses in Emotional Storms

When waves of doubt crash on the shore,
We stand as beacons, we're forevermore.
Through darkest nights, we guide the way,
With every heartbeat, we choose to stay.

In tempests fierce, our lights won't fade,
Our voices rise, a serenade.
We weather storms with hands held tight,
In unity, we find our light.

The lighthouse gleams, a steadfast sign,
That hope endures, our hearts align.
In turbulent seas, we trust the call,
With compassion strong, we'll never fall.

Through raging winds and thunder loud,
We stand as one, forever proud.
As lighthouses, we shine so bright,
In emotional storms, we're each other's light.

Silhouettes of Understanding

In shadows cast from hearts so wide,
We find the truths we cannot hide.
Each silhouette tells tales untold,
In quiet moments, we feel so bold.

With every line, we sketch our fears,
In understanding, we dry our tears.
The forms we take, they shift and sway,
Our dance of life, come what may.

In softening light, we see the grace,
Of every soul, in this vast space.
The whispers echo, silent sighs,
In silhouettes, our bond complies.

Through every curve, connections bloom,
In every gap, we find room.
With open hearts, we stand aligned,
In the art of love, we grow combined.

Reflections in a Shared Heart

In the mirror of your eyes,
I see dreams softly glow,
Flickers of a shared past,
In whispers only we know.

Two minds dance in the twilight,
Echoing secrets like stars,
Every heartbeat a melody,
Binding us near, never far.

Through valleys deep we wander,
Hand in hand, side by side,
Every laughter a testament,
To a love we cannot hide.

In silence, our souls converse,
Woven tales of joy and tears,
Reflections caught in moments,
A tapestry of our years.

As seasons change and shift,
Love's anthem plays anew,
In the mirror of your heart,
I find my home in you.

Ripples of Kindness

Splash of a smile, so gentle,
A wave in the ocean vast,
Kindness flows like a river,
Touching lives, present and past.

Every gesture, a pebble tossed,
Creating rings in the air,
With each act of pure giving,
Hope blooms brightly everywhere.

In the quiet of the morning,
An opening heart sings loud,
Bridging gaps with soft whispers,
Together we stand, so proud.

From neighbors to strangers,
A thread that binds us tight,
Through ripples of compassion,
We illuminate the night.

So let kindness be our anthem,
In a world that longs to heal,
Small acts with great intention,
Together, our hearts reveal.

Resonance of Souls

In the hush where shadows play,
Two hearts tune to a song,
Rhythms align in the starlight,
Where we both truly belong.

The universe hums our chorus,
Each note a gentle embrace,
In the silence, we are echoes,
Finding color in the space.

Whispers dance on the breeze,
Carrying dreams through the night,
A symphony of intentions,
Crafted in love's pure light.

Moments may flicker and fade,
Yet our bond remains strong,
In the melody of existence,
Together, we'll sing along.

As the stars weave between us,
A connection deeply sown,
In the resonance of our souls,
We forever are not alone.

When Heartstrings Align

In the silence of the moonlight,
Two hearts begin to play,
Strumming chords of understanding,
In the softest, sweetest way.

When laughter echoes freely,
And our dreams begin to soar,
The world fades into the background,
As we discover so much more.

With each shared glance, electric,
A dance of spirits unfold,
Every heartbeat syncs in time,
Stories of love retold.

Through valleys and over mountains,
Our passion lights the way,
Binding threads of our journeys,
In the tapestry we lay.

As the stars watch our duet,
In the universe's design,
Forever will we be woven,
When our heartstrings align.

The Light in Another's Darkness

In shadows deep, a flicker glows,
A hand reaches out, where kindness grows.
In quiet spaces, hope is found,
A gentle whisper, love unbound.

Through the night, we share the weight,
A bond of souls, we elevate.
Your pain reflects, a mirror bright,
Together we stand, igniting light.

When storms arise, when fears untold,
We rise as one, courageous and bold.
In darkest times, we find our path,
With hearts of fire, we conquer wrath.

In brokenness, beauty lies,
We lift each other, 'neath the skies.
With every tear, a story shared,
In unity, we find we're cared.

So let us walk through night and gloom,
With love in heart, we'll chase the doom.
For in the dark, we shine more bright,
As hand in hand, we bring the light.

Kindred Spirits in Solitude

In quiet corners, souls align,
Through whispers soft, our hearts entwine.
In stillness found, we breathe the air,
A gentle peace, a bond so rare.

We sail alone, yet not apart,
For in our silence, beats one heart.
The world may fade, but we endure,
With kindred spirits, strong and pure.

Through evening shades, we tread with grace,
Embracing light in this sacred space.
With every glance, a knowing glance,
In shared stillness, we find our chance.

When shadows linger, we stand tall,
Encouraging whispers, we will not fall.
Together we rise, in softest hue,
Two souls as one, forever true.

In solitude, we find the way,
To love unspoken, come what may.
Together we weave, a tapestry bright,
In kindred spirits, we take flight.

Lessons in Vulnerability

In tender moments, truth reveals,
A brave heart opens, pain it feels.
With fragile voice, we share our scars,
In vulnerability, we find the stars.

Through every tear, a lesson learned,
In cracks of silence, wisdom burned.
For courage blooms in softened gaze,
When walls come down, we learn to praise.

With every word, we break the chains,
In honest touch, the heart still gains.
Embracing fears, the shadows wane,
In open hearts, we heal the pain.

In whispered trust, connections grow,
Through shared experience, our spirits flow.
In stories told, we find the light,
In lessons learned, we take our flight.

So let us speak, let hearts unfold,
In vulnerability, brave and bold.
For in our truth, a dance of grace,
In every moment, we find our place.

Heartbeats in Harmony

In rhythm shared, our spirits sing,
A melody of love takes wing.
With every pulse, our hearts align,
In perfect time, our souls entwine.

Through laughter bright, and tears we share,
In every moment, love laid bare.
With gentle beats, we move as one,
Creating tunes that can't be undone.

When life gets hard, we hold on tight,
Together we weather, day and night.
In harmony, we find our way,
Each heartbeat echoes, 'come what may.'

With open arms, we face the storm,
In deepest love, we stay warm.
Through changes vast, we still remain,
In every heartbeat, love's sweet refrain.

Let music play, let spirit dance,
In every glance, we take a chance.
For with each heartbeat, song's embrace,
In harmony, we find our place.

Murmurs in the Dark

Whispers roam the midnight air,
Secrets pass between the trees.
Soft shadows dance without a care,
Echoes linger in the breeze.

Stars are dimmed by thoughts unspoken,
Dreams unfold as night descends.
Hearts once tender now lay broken,
Finding solace where it ends.

The moon provides a muted glow,
Guiding lost souls on their way.
In silence, deeper feelings flow,
Murmurs linger, never stray.

Fingers trace the lines of fate,
In the dark, we find our tune.
Bound by the weight of love and hate,
Our stories sing beneath the moon.

Each breath carries a tender sigh,
Wrapped in warmth, we seek and yearn.
In this dusk, we learn to fly,
In this dark, our hearts still burn.

Embracing Another's Shadow

In the light, we stand apart,
Yet your shadow holds me tight.
Yearning whispers stir the heart,
In the silence, I find light.

Weaving close through sun and shade,
Every breath, an echo made.
In your presence, fears do fade,
Together, we dance unafraid.

Moments wrapped in timeless grace,
In your warmth, I find my place.
Every glance, a sweet embrace,
We become a softened space.

Beneath the stars, our secrets blend,
Two souls swirling, fate is penned.
Through the storm, you are my friend,
In the dark, our hearts defend.

As we stroll through smiles and tears,
Hand in hand, we face our fears.
In this bond, love perseveres,
Embracing shadows through the years.

Threads of Human Experience

In every heartbeat, stories weave,
A tapestry of shared delight.
From whispered dreams to lessons grieved,
Each thread shines bright in the night.

Love and loss dance hand in hand,
Tender moments softly sewn.
Deep connections, a symphonic band,
Together, we're never alone.

Paths crossed in a fleeting glance,
Each encounter leaves a mark.
In this life, we take a chance,
Finding beauty in the dark.

Joy resounds in laughter's spell,
The weight of sorrow finds its place.
Within our stories, we can tell,
Life's fleeting threads we now embrace.

As time flows on like a gentle stream,
Each memory becomes a thread.
Together, we follow the gleam,
In the fabric of love, we spread.

Notes of Shared Struggle

In the shadows where we dwell,
Voices rise to break the night.
Echoes of the tales we tell,
Together, we search for light.

In the struggle, hearts unite,
A chorus built from pain and pride.
Through the darkness, we find might,
Standing strong, side by side.

Moments stained by tears we weep,
Yet resilience finds its song.
In our grief, we plant and reap,
Creating roots, we grow strong.

The melodies of change resound,
With every step, a chance to rise.
In this path, our hope is found,
Together, we reach for skies.

Not alone in battles fought,
Hand in hand, we light the way.
In this movement, love is sought,
Notes of struggle, here we stay.

Portraits of Kindness Unseen

In shadows where the small acts dwell,
A smile exchanged, a whispered tell.
Hands reach out in silent grace,
Creating warmth in a cold place.

The gentle touch of a knowing glance,
Inviting hearts to shift and dance.
In the unnoticed, love does bloom,
Filling quietly every room.

Lifting spirits with unseen might,
Giving hope a chance to ignite.
Each kindness cast, a ripple wide,
In the depths where shadows hide.

Through small gestures, bonds are formed,
In the quiet, hearts are warmed.
For every soul that gives a part,
Creates a portrait of the heart.

So let us weave this tapestry,
Of unseen acts, a symphony.
In every thread, a story spun,
Of kindness shared, two souls as one.

Echoing Hearts

In every heartbeat, a story lives,
Tales of courage, love that gives.
Whispers travel on the breeze,
Uniting souls with gentle ease.

Echoes bounce from heart to heart,
A symphony of life's fine art.
In laughter's ring, we find our tune,
Two melodies beneath the moon.

Every sigh, each shared delight,
Becomes a guiding star at night.
Filling spaces where silence grew,
With all the dreams we dare pursue.

In tender moments, we will find,
The ties that wrap and gently bind.
An echo lingers, soft and clear,
A heartbeat close, that we hold dear.

From whispered vows to shouts of joy,
Life's harmony we'll both employ.
With every pulse, our spirits soar,
In echoing hearts forever more.

Luminescence of Shared Laughter

In the glow of shared delight,
Laughter dances, pure and bright.
Like stars that twinkle in the night,
Moments captured, hearts take flight.

With every chuckle, shadows fade,
Building bridges, fears evade.
In joyous echoes, spirits blend,
A tapestry with no end.

Jokes spun like threads, finely weaved,
In laughter's warmth, we are believed.
Creating bonds that never break,
A melody that we all make.

Every giggle, a spark of light,
Transforming darkness into sight.
In shared moments, we can see,
The luminescence of you and me.

Through laughter's lens, the world feels new,
Each joy a treasure, bright and true.
In the light of smiles, we discover,
A shared warmth like none other.

Fables of Soft Resilience

In whispers of the winds that sigh,
Tales of strength in hearts that cry.
Like gentle blooms that break through stone,
Stories rise where hope has grown.

Each chapter etched in lines of grace,
Resilience blooms in every space.
Through storms that rattle, roots hold tight,
Fables written in the light.

With every fall, a rise anew,
The courage found when skies turn blue.
In softness lies a thund'rous might,
A secret strength in starry night.

For every tear that paints the past,
A lesson learned, a love amassed.
In gentle waves, we find our way,
Soft resilience here to stay.

So let the tales of strength be told,
In hearts of silver, dreams of gold.
For every struggle, every fight,
Creates a story, pure delight.

The Undercurrent of Togetherness

In quiet whispers, we unite,
A tapestry of dreams in sight.
With hands entwined, we find our way,
In shadows cast, we greet the day.

A dance of souls, a gentle sigh,
Through trials faced, we learn to fly.
The bonds we forge, a silent pact,
In every heartbeat, love's impact.

With laughter bright, we share our fears,
In every glance, a world appears.
Together strong, we break the mold,
In warmth and grace, our stories told.

In moments shared, true strength we find,
An undercurrent, pure and kind.
Through stormy seas and tranquil nights,
We sail as one, our spirits' flights.

In every tear and every smile,
Together we walk, mile by mile.
A bond unbroken, fierce and free,
The undercurrent of unity.

Harmonies of the Heart

In melodies soft, our hearts align,
A symphony beneath the pine.
With echoes sweet, we weave our song,
In perfect rhythms, we belong.

Each note a spark, igniting fire,
In laughter shared, we rise higher.
The whispers low, the crescendos soar,
In harmonies, we find our core.

With hands held tight, we reach for dreams,
In every moment, love redeems.
Our voices blend in vibrant hue,
In symphonic waves, forever true.

Through trials faced, we hold the tune,
Amidst the stars, beneath the moon.
A chorus rich, a heart entwined,
In harmonies, our souls aligned.

As dusk descends and shadows play,
We sing together, night and day.
In sacred sounds, we share our part,
A timeless dance, harmonies of heart.

A Symphony of Solace

In quietude, we find our breath,
A symphony that conquers death.
With soft refrains, the heart does heal,
In echoes low, we start to feel.

Through gentle notes of sweet embrace,
In solitude, we find our space.
Each chord a balm, each silence deep,
In symphony, our sorrows sleep.

With aching strings and soothing sound,
In every pause, our hopes abound.
The melodies drift, the dawn awakes,
In harmony, our spirit breaks.

Together in the quiet night,
We find our way, reclaim our light.
In whispers soft, we rise above,
A symphony woven from our love.

Each heart a note, each soul a score,
In solace found, we seek for more.
A symphony where pain subsides,
In every note, our truth abides.

Glimmers of Compassionate Light

In darkest hours, a flicker shines,
A beacon bright where kindness binds.
With tender hearts, we share our plight,
Glimmers of love, compassionate light.

Through winding paths, we show the way,
In every smile, a brighter day.
With open arms, we bridge the space,
In acts of grace, we find our place.

Each gentle gesture, a soothing balm,
In storms of life, we bring the calm.
The light we share, a sacred flame,
In unity, we know no shame.

In simple words, our hopes ignite,
With every step, we fight the fight.
For in our hearts, a truth takes flight,
Glimmers of warmth, compassionate light.

Together strong, we rise anew,
In every dawn, we dare to pursue.
A world transformed, love's endless height,
In glimmers bright, we find our might.

Echoes of a Shared Journey

In the twilight glow, we walk side by side,
Each step a whisper, where dreams coincide.
With laughter like echoes, the past floats around,
Memories woven, in silence profound.

Through valleys of shadows, our courage takes flight,
In moments of stillness, we embrace the night.
Hand in hand always, we face the unknown,
In the songs of our hearts, we find our home.

The stars tell our stories, of journeys untold,
We gather together, as destinies unfold.
With the map of our spirits, we carve our own way,
In the dance of the present, we choose to stay.

Each challenge a lesson, in the light of the dawn,
We rise through the trials, though the road may be long.
Forever we travel, through laughter and tears,
In the echoes of friendship, we conquer our fears.

The Softness of One's Struggles

In the quiet of twilight, soft shadows descend,
A tender reflection, where hearts often mend.
Behind every smile, a story resides,
Of battles fought bravely, where solace abides.

Each tear that has fallen, a lesson in grace,
In the depths of our struggles, we learn to embrace.
With courage, we gather the pieces in hand,
And find strength in the softness, where dreams make their stand.

When heavy hearts wander, in search of the light,
It's the warmth of connection that makes darkness bright.
Through whispers of comfort, we rise from the dust,
In the softness of struggle, we place all our trust.

Bound by our journey, we share in the pain,
Through storms and the sunshine, our souls weave a chain.
The tapestry woven, with threads of pure gold,
Speaks of love and compassion, stories retold.

Bridges Between Heartbeats

In the rhythm of moments, connections arise,
Bridges we build through the echoing sighs.
With each heartbeat spoken, a story unfolds,
Uniting our spirits in warmth to behold.

Across the vast silence, our voices ignite,
Creating a pathway to dreams taking flight.
With trust as our anchor, we soar through the skies,
In the quietest corners, true love never lies.

When shadows grow longer, and doubts start to creep,
We find in each other the strength that we keep.
With every heartbeat, a promise we make,
Together we wander, whatever it takes.

In the fragile moments, when hope feels so thin,
We nurture the bridges that help us begin.
With laughter as lanterns, we light up the dark,
And dance on the bridges, our souls leave a mark.

Songs of Hidden Pain

In the depths of silence, a melody hums,
A song of despair, where the heart slowly drums.
With shadows as witnesses, we whisper our fears,
In the cadence of heartache, we drown out our tears.

Each note carries burdens, unspoken, they ache,
In harmonies woven, the fragile hearts break.
Through the verses of sorrow, we find our refrain,
In the echoes of anguish, we dance with the pain.

Yet, within that darkness, a flicker of light,
In tunes of resilience, we learn to ignite.
With voices united, we conquer the night,
Our songs of survival, a powerful sight.

For beyond the hidden, the beauty does flow,
In the depth of our struggles, our strength starts to grow.
And as we sing louder, the pain drifts away,
In the heart of our music, new hopes find their way.

Fountains of Mutual Care

In gardens green where blossoms sway,
We share our joys, the light of day.
With tender hands, we plant our seeds,
In friendship's soil, we meet our needs.

Laughter flows like streams so clear,
In moments spent, we hold what's dear.
Through gentle words and quiet grace,
We weave a bond time can't erase.

As shadows fall and twilight nears,
We gather close to conquer fears.
Each heartbeat echoes strong and true,
In every smile, a love renews.

When storms arise and tempests roar,
Our trust will guide, forevermore.
In unity, we'll face the fight,
Together, we shall find the light.

So let us drink from friendship's cup,
In fountains deep, we lift each up.
With open hearts, we'll always share,
The endless gift of mutual care.

Outcries of Silent Struggles

In whispered tones, the truth is found,
Beneath the surface, battles bound.
With heavy hearts, we walk alone,
Yet in our eyes, the pain is shown.

The sleepless nights, the weight we bear,
In crowded rooms, we're often bare.
Yet silent cries can pierce the air,
A strength within, a fragile flare.

Through hidden scars and battles waged,
We find our voice, though still we're caged.
Each story told, a step toward light,
In shared confessions, we ignite.

The price of silence, hard to pay,
Yet hope can bloom in shades of gray.
In kindness shared, our burdens ease,
Together, we can find our peace.

So let us speak, unshackle pain,
Through shared outcries, we will gain.
In unity, our strength will grow,
In silent struggles, love will flow.

Echoes of Shared Stories

In tales retold around the fire,
We find our hearts and hope aspire.
Each whispered secret, woven tight,
Creates a tapestry of light.

From distant lands and times long past,
Our stories bind, forever cast.
The joys and sorrows that we've shared,
In every word, we've always cared.

Through laughter's echo, tears may fall,
Each chapter tells, unites us all.
The power held in voice and pen,
Brings near the souls of distant kin.

For in this world both wide and vast,
The threads of love and hurt are cast.
We gather 'round, our stories glow,
In unity, our spirits flow.

So let us write, let voices rise,
In echoes clear beneath the skies.
Together now, we share our song,
In stories shared, we all belong.

Murmurs of the Heart

In quiet moments, whispers speak,
With gentle tones, our souls will seek.
A tender touch, a knowing glance,
In every heartbeat, love's expanse.

The murmur soft like rustling leaves,
In sacred trust, our spirit cleaves.
With every sigh, the world we share,
In hushed confessions, truths laid bare.

As twilight paints the skies in hue,
We find the peace in me and you.
In laughter bright and tears that gleam,
We share our dreams, we dare to dream.

Through trials faced and triumphs won,
Our journeys blend, we rise as one.
In every murmur, hearts connect,
In tender love, we all reflect.

So listen close, let silence reign,
In whispered hopes, we'll ease the pain.
In murmur's grace, we shall find way,
To hold each other come what may.

Harmonies of Care and Trust

In whispers shared beneath the stars,
Laughter echoes, healing scars.
With every glance, a bond we weave,
In care and trust, we choose to believe.

Hand in hand through thick and thin,
Together we grow, together we win.
In gentle words, our spirits rise,
In each other's gaze, we find our skies.

A mosaic of stories, vividly bright,
Each note composed in soft twilight.
In vulnerable moments, we find our way,
With hearts entwined, come what may.

The dance of friendship, graceful and true,
In every rhythm, I find you.
Harmony flourishes, notes intertwine,
In the symphony of care, we shine.

Through trials faced, hands remain clasped,
A fortress of trust, no joy missed.
In the embrace of warmth, fears disappear,
Together we thrive, year after year.

Emanations of Mutual Respect

In shadows cast, light softly gleams,
Respect blooms in shared dreams.
With every voice, a truth takes flight,
In the embrace of equals, everything feels right.

Acknowledgment flows like gentle streams,
In the garden of thought, we nurture our dreams.
Each perspective honored, we learn and grow,
In the dance of respect, seeds of trust sow.

Boundaries set, yet hearts stay wide,
In every story, we take pride.
Listening deeply, we carve our space,
In mutual respect, we find our grace.

With open minds, we build a bridge,
Navigating waters, we never smidge.
In the tapestry woven with threads of care,
In love and respect, we choose to share.

Emanations rise from each spoken word,
In the chorus of kindness, our voices are heard.
Together we flourish, undeterred by strife,
In this sacred bond, we cherish life.

Firesides of Gentle Conversations

By the warm glow of flickering light,
We share our dreams, our fears take flight.
In the hush of night, our secrets unfold,
In gentle tones, our stories told.

With every ember, warmth ignites,
In the embrace of shadows, we find delights.
In laughter shared and silences deep,
Fireside chats, memories to keep.

We weave our thoughts like threads of yarn,
In the tapestry of trust, we feel reborn.
Every whisper soft, every sigh pure,
In these sacred moments, we find our cure.

As sparks dance high, our visions align,
In the space between, our hearts entwine.
With every flicker, a bond we create,
By the fireside, love radiates.

Through shifting winds, our flames may sway,
But together we stand, come what may.
In gentle conversations, our spirits soar,
By the fireside's glow, forevermore.

Luminaries of Emotional Support

In the darkest hours, a beacon shines,
Illuminating paths, crossing our minds.
With every touch, a warmth bestowed,
In emotional support, seeds of hope grow.

Hand on shoulder, hearts entwined,
In shared silence, peace we find.
When shadows linger and spirits wane,
Together we rise, through joy and pain.

Cascades of love, like moonlit beams,
In the fabric of friendship, we stitch our dreams.
With every word, the night feels less long,
In the choir of courage, our voices strong.

Through storms we weather, hand in hand,
In the gardens of trust, we firmly stand.
With empathy as our guiding light,
We offer solace through every night.

Luminaries shining, hearts aglow,
In the warmth of compassion, our spirits flow.
Together we flourish, forever to stand,
In the glow of support, side by side, hand in hand.

Chronicles of Togetherness

In quiet moments, we find our place,
Hand in hand, we face the space.
Laughter echoes through shared air,
In every glance, a tender care.

Step by step, our stories weave,
In the warmth, we're meant to believe.
Through storms and calm, side by side,
In our hearts, love can't abide.

With every dream, we build a bridge,
As we dance along life's ridge.
Our voices blend, a soothing song,
In this journey, we belong.

Time unfolds its gentle grace,
In every challenge, we embrace.
Together strong, we rise and grow,
In unity, our spirits glow.

We carve our names in the sands of time,
With hopes and dreams that gently climb.
In the chapters of our fate,
Together, we create, we narrate.

Waves of Shared Humanity

Across the shore, our hearts collide,
In every wave, our fears subside.
With open arms, we share this land,
In unity, we take a stand.

Voices rise like the morning tide,
In every struggle, we confide.
Through laughter's sparkle, tears that flow,
Together, we learn and grow.

Beneath the stars, our dreams ignite,
In shared stories, we find the light.
From different paths, we come as one,
In this symphony, we have fun.

In fleeting moments, we take a breath,
Finding strength in love, not death.
A tapestry of life we weave,
In the quiet, we believe.

In kindness shown, we break the chains,
In this dance, love remains.
With every heartbeat, together we sway,
In waves of hope, we find our way.

Flavors of Compassionate Dialogue

In every word, a taste of grace,
Through open hearts, we share space.
With gentle tones, we learn to speak,
In understanding, we find the peak.

Conversations rich, like spices blend,
In every story, we can mend.
From different walks, we gather near,
In every voice, a song to hear.

With patience, we savor each sound,
In shared silence, love is found.
Through laughter and tears, we engage,
In this moment, we turn the page.

Compassion flows like a fragrant breeze,
In harmony, we find our ease.
With open minds, we bridge the gaps,
In every meeting, there's no mishaps.

In flavors deep, we taste the truth,
In dialogue, we nurture youth.
With every exchange, connections grow,
In every heart, compassion glows.

Reflections on a Shared Path

Along this trail, our footsteps blend,
In each reflection, we transcend.
With eyes wide open, hearts unsealed,
In shared journeys, we are healed.

Through winding roads and valleys low,
In every twist, we come to know.
With stories told, we pave the way,
In this memory, we choose to stay.

A tapestry of dreams we weave,
In each moment, we believe.
With hands held tight, we face the fight,
In shared hopes, we find the light.

In laughter's ring, in silence deep,
In every promise, secrets keep.
Through challenges met, we rise anew,
In unity found, our spirits grew.

So let us walk, side by side,
In every heartbeat, love as our guide.
Through reflecting on paths we've trod,
In each other, we find our God.

A Cradle of Kindred Spirits

In twilight's glow, we gather near,
Soft whispers dance, where hearts draw clear.
Fingers entwined, in comfort's hold,
A tapestry rich, in stories told.

Laughter spills like sunlight's grace,
Through shared journeys, we find our space.
Roots intertwined, in sacred ground,
In this cradle, love's echo found.

With every smile, we weave a thread,
In kindness sown, where none shall tread.
Together we rise, in life's soft quilt,
A sanctuary built, in warmth and tilt.

As shadows pass, and seasons change,
Our bond remains, though paths may range.
In every heart, a kindred spark,
We light the world, together, dark.

Through storms we stand, both strong and free,
In unity, our spirit's decree.
With open arms, we face the night,
In this cradle, we find our light.

Glimpses of Hidden Pain

Behind the smile, a shadow creeps,
A silent battle, where sorrow sleeps.
Eyes that twinkle, hearts that break,
Through whispered secrets, the walls will quake.

In crowded rooms, the silence sings,
The weight of longing, the ghost of springs.
A fragile mask, we wear with grace,
Yet inside lies a hidden place.

Through every joke, a longing sigh,
The laughter flows, but tears still lie.
We share our woes in subtle cues,
In fragments of hearts, the truth imbues.

In shadows cast, resilience grows,
Each silent wound, the spirit knows.
In quiet moments, the heart finds peace,
Through glimpses shared, the pain may cease.

So lift the veil, let feelings show,
For in our honesty, the warmth will flow.
Through shared compassion, we start to heal,
Transforming pain into something real.

Threads of Shared Humanity

In the tapestry of life, we thread,
A vibrant mix of paths we've led.
Each story told, a glimpse, a share,
In our differences, we find the rare.

From every corner, voices blend,
In the chorus, together we mend.
Through laughter brought, and sorrow known,
In every heart, a seed is sown.

The ties that bind are often unseen,
Yet in our souls, they form the green.
With gentle hands, we weave strong ties,
In the fabric of life, love never dies.

Through every struggle, we hold the light,
Together we rise, in shared might.
Each heartbeat echoes, a rhythmic song,
In unity found, where we all belong.

In our diversity, we find the gold,
In the stories of old, and tales untold.
Threads woven tight, in harmony spun,
In the quilt of humanity, we are one.

Kaleidoscope of Emotions

In the prism of life, colors collide,
A dance of feelings, we cannot hide.
Joy flickers bright, like stars on high,
While shades of sadness quietly sigh.

Anger flares like a stormy sky,
Passion ignites, making spirits fly.
In the depths of fear, we find our strength,
Through cycles of love, we grow in length.

Hope shines like gold, in darkest days,
A guiding light, in myriad ways.
With every tear, a rainbow forms,
In every heart, a fire warms.

As joy and sorrow intertwine,
The dance of life, a sacred sign.
In every heartbeat, emotions play,
A kaleidoscope brightens the day.

We weave our tales, both bold and meek,
In the spectrum of life, we seek.
Through love and loss, we find our way,
In this kaleidoscope, we learn to stay.

The Secret Language of Sorrow

In whispers soft, the shadows creep,
Where silent tears and secrets keep.
A heart once whole, now torn apart,
Echoes linger in the dark.

Each sigh a tale, each breath a pain,
A symphony of loss, a gentle rain.
Unspoken words crave to be free,
Yet remain trapped in memory.

The night conceals what day reveals,
Hidden hurts, the heart congeals.
In solitude, the truth stands bare,
In the world's noise, none seem to care.

Yet in this anguish, beauty lies,
A fragile strength that never dies.
From ruins rise the weary souls,
Binding wounds in silent roles.

In every crack, a light will gleam,
The secret language, a waking dream.
Through sorrow's depths, we find our way,
In healing's touch, we learn to stay.

Hearts that Speak

In fleeting glances, worlds collide,
Two hearts find rhythm, side by side.
A silent language softly plays,
In gentle smiles, the warmth stays.

Words unspoken weave a thread,
Connecting souls, where silence led.
In tender moments, time stands still,
A dance of hearts, a shared will.

The eyes can echo what lips won't say,
In every heartbeat, love finds its way.
With every touch, a story starts,
In the quiet, we become art.

Through laughter shared and tears embraced,
These precious ties can't be replaced.
In the night's hush, our spirits soar,
Two hearts that speak, forevermore.

No grand display could match this grace,
In simple truths, we find our place.
A language sweet, unrefined,
A treasure in the love we find.

Fleeting Moments of Connection

A smiling glance across the room,
A spark ignites, dispelling gloom.
In transient seconds, souls entwine,
An echo of what could be mine.

The laughter shared, a brief embrace,
In crowded spaces, we leave a trace.
Moments pass like whispers in flight,
Yet linger deeply through the night.

A fleeting brush, a touch divine,
In this chaos, hearts align.
Life's tapestry of chance and fate,
We bind our stories, celebrate.

Time may steal what we hold dear,
But echoes of laughter, we keep near.
Each precious moment, a timeless song,
In fleeting connections, we belong.

Though paths may part, the heart will know,
The beauty found in the overflow.
In every glance and shared delight,
Fleeting moments become our light.

Mending in the Silence

In quiet hours, the heart finds peace,
In stillness, moments seem to cease.
Where chaos fades, and thoughts align,
We heal the wounds, the hearts entwine.

The gentle touch, a soothing balm,
In silence wrapped, it feels so calm.
With every breath, our spirits mend,
In hushed embraces, love transcends.

Beneath the weight of world's demand,
We hold each other, hand in hand.
The unspoken truth, a gentle guide,
In this calm, our fears subside.

Restoring souls with every pause,
A beauty found in love's own cause.
In the absence of words, we see
The power in stillness, you and me.

Together we stand, as silence speaks,
In the quiet moments, love's heart seeks.
Mending softly, as shadows dance,
In this sacred space, we find our chance.

Beyond the Surface

Beneath the calm, the waters churn,
Secrets hide, waiting to return.
Reflections dance in light's embrace,
Yet depths conceal a hidden space.

Bubbles rise, thoughts that expand,
Every whisper, a wave so grand.
Dive deeper still, let shadows play,
In darkness, truths find their way.

A silver shell hides pearls inside,
The heart's true song it always hides.
Unlock the door, let courage swell,
For in the depths, we find our shell.

Each ripple tells a story's part,
Of love, of loss, of every heart.
So look beyond what eyes can see,
And find the depths that set you free.

A Hand to Hold

In quiet moments, hands entwine,
A simple touch, a loving sign.
Through storms and sun, they guide the way,
A hand to hold, come what may.

With gentle strength, they lift the fall,
In silent screams, they hear it all.
A lifeline stretched, a warm embrace,
In every heartbeat, love finds its place.

Together facing shadows' fright,
They stand as one, a glowing light.
In laughter shared and tears consoled,
The magic lies in hands to hold.

Through paths of joy and sorrows steep,
The bond grows strong, the promise deep.
So take a hand, let spirits soar,
In unity, we find our core.

Exploring Unseen Wounds

Beneath the smiles, the laughter's glow,
Lie scars unseen, hidden below.
In silence, stories weave and twine,
Exploring wounds that intertwine.

Each heartbeat echoes of battles fought,
In shadows cast by lessons taught.
A tender touch, a gentle gaze,
Can soothe the ache of darker days.

With courage built, we face the past,
Understanding brings a peace that lasts.
Through open hearts, let healing start,
In shared pain, we find our art.

So hold the light, and walk the path,
Through unseen wounds, there's love to bath.
Exploring depths, we freely roam,
In every scar, we find our home.

When Two Souls Meet

In whispered winds, two souls collide,
A hidden spark they cannot hide.
Familiar warmth, a comforting glow,
In stillness found, their spirits flow.

Like rivers merging into one,
They dance beneath the setting sun.
In every glance, a thousand tales,
Their journey starts where love prevails.

In laughter shared and quiet sighs,
They find a haven, no goodbyes.
Together painting dreams anew,
In vibrant hues, a love so true.

With each heartbeat, their rhythm thrums,
In softest echoes, joy becomes.
When two souls meet, the world feels right,
For in their bond, they share the light.

Chords of Collective Feeling

In shadows deep, a whisper flows,
Where hearts align, a warmth bestows.
Together we rise, through darkest night,
In harmony's breath, we find our light.

Lifting each other, we stand as one,
In the song of us, no need to run.
Each note a bond, a shared refrain,
Resounding softly, easing the pain.

With every strum, the world expands,
A melody written in joining hands.
Through laughter and tears, we weave our fate,
United in peace as we resonate.

The echoes linger, sweet and strong,
In the chords we sing, we all belong.
A tapestry rich, in colors bright,
Together we shine, a brilliant sight.

So let us play, let our spirits soar,
In this symphony, forevermore.
With every heartbeat, let love reveal,
The chords of collective feeling, so real.

Beneath the Surface of Hurt

Beneath the veil, the shadows creep,
In silence held, our secrets we keep.
Pain etched softly in the eyes,
A hidden world, where sorrow lies.

Yet in those depths, a spark remains,
Whispers of courage, breaking chains.
We wade through rivers, cold and wide,
Finding the solace that pain can hide.

Each tear a story, each scar a song,
In the journey of healing, we learn to be strong.
With hands clasped tight, and hearts exposed,
To rise from ashes, love is proposed.

Those wounds, they teach us, guide us through,
To embrace the shadows, to find what's true.
Emerging brighter, with every scar,
The beauty we carry reveals who we are.

So let us dive, uncover the core,
With every breath, we'll seek for more.
Through the depths of hurt, we will see,
The strength in the journey, the heart's decree.

Songs of Silent Understanding

In quiet moments, our eyes will meet,
A language spoken, bittersweet.
No words are needed, we just know,
In shared silence, our feelings grow.

The gentle nod, the subtle glance,
In this stillness, we find our chance.
To weave a bond, unbreakable thread,
In every heartbeat, unsaid, widespread.

Through storms we walk, hand in hand,
In the silence, together we stand.
With every breath, an unvoiced song,
A rhythm that binds us, steadfast and strong.

The world may rush, but here we pause,
In this quiet, we find our cause.
For in the silence, a truth will speak,
A testament to the love we seek.

So let us cherish this sacred space,
In understanding, a warm embrace.
Through uncharted realms, together we'll glide,
In songs of silence, our hearts collide.

Reverberations of Caring

In every touch, a gentle spark,
The flame of hope, igniting the dark.
With kindness shared, the world expands,
In reverberations, we make our stands.

The warmth of hearts, through distance felt,
In shared compassion, a bond is dealt.
Through every gesture, love finds its way,
In the echoes of caring, we choose to stay.

With words unspoken, we feel the call,
To lift each other, to never fall.
In moments shared, our spirits soar,
In reverberations, worth fighting for.

The kindness ripples, like a silent stream,
In hearts entwined, we chase the dream.
In laughter and tears, we rise and fall,
In the dance of caring, we give our all.

So let us spread this warmth around,
In every heart, let love be found.
For in the echoes, we shall discover,
The true power of each other.

Whispers of Compassion

In the silence, kindness breathes,
Soft murmurs in the night,
Gentle hands that lift the load,
A shared warmth, pure delight.

Eyes that sparkle with true care,
Echoes of a tender heart,
In every moment, we reach out,
Compassion's art, a sacred part.

Through the shadows, light will shine,
In every story, souls entwined,
Together we can brave the storms,
With whispered hopes, we are aligned.

Bridges built on trust and love,
In the heart's embrace, we grow,
The world is brighter, hand in hand,
Compassion's seeds, together sow.

As we journey, side by side,
Every step a promise sweet,
In the whispers of the night,
Our hearts make the world complete.

Reflections of Heartstrings

In the mirror of our eyes,
Stories dance, shadows gleam,
Threads of fate tightly woven,
In every breath, a dream.

With each heartbeat, rhythms clash,
Harmony in disarray,
Yet through echoes of our strife,
Together, we find our way.

Reflecting truth in fragile glass,
Tender moments, pure and rare,
Heartstrings tug, connections deep,
In silent vows, we lay bare.

The melody of love resounds,
In the laughter, in the tears,
Knotted threads that hold us close,
Bringing solace to our fears.

With every glance, a spark ignites,
In the warmth of what we feel,
The world transforms with love's embrace,
In each reflection, dreams reveal.

Resonance of Understanding

In the depths of silence still,
Whispers weave a bond so tight,
Hearts attuned, a gentle beat,
In the dark, we find our light.

Eyes that echo stories told,
Each gaze a window to the soul,
Through the fog of life's journey,
Understanding makes us whole.

In the moments shared, we grow,
Empathy, a powerful thread,
With every word, a bridge we build,
Uniting voices in what's said.

Through the laughter and the pain,
Resonance rings, a sacred song,
In the dance of shared existence,
Together we forge where we belong.

With every heartbeat, we align,
In the rhythm, we find grace,
Understanding blooms like spring,
In this vast, embracing space.

Tides of Shared Grief

In the depths of sorrow's sea,
Waves of longing ebb and flow,
Together we navigate the storm,
In shared grief, our hearts glow.

Each tear a beacon, shining bright,
Guiding us through darkest nights,
In the silence, hand in hand,
We find solace, endless flights.

Echoes linger in the still,
Resonating with memories,
In the hush of whispered pain,
Love's embrace brings gentle ease.

As the tides of healing rise,
Carrying hopes upon the shore,
In the depths of our despair,
Together, our spirits soar.

Through the losses, we unite,
In fragility, we're alive,
In the tides of shared grief,
Together we learn to thrive.

The Fabric of Shared Humanity

In every heart there lies a thread,
Woven tight with love and dread.
Colors blend, a tapestry,
Reflecting hopes for all to see.

From distant shores and lands unknown,
We share a pain, we share a tone.
In laughter's echo, in sorrow's song,
Together, we find where we belong.

With open hands and hearts alight,
We build a bridge, we find the light.
In unity, our strength will bloom,
Dispelling shadows, conquering gloom.

To understand is to embrace,
The varied paths that we all trace.
Threads entwined, we rise as one,
A symphony beneath the sun.

So let us weave with tender care,
A fabric rich, beyond compare.
In every stitch, a story shared,
In every fold, a life declared.

Amidst the Cries for Connection

In crowded rooms, we seek a glance,
A fleeting moment, a whispered chance.
Among the noise, our voices blend,
Yearning hearts, longing to mend.

Through screens we search, with fingers crossed,
Hoping to find what feels not lost.
In messages and emojis bright,
We chase the shadows, reach for light.

Yet silence speaks in loudest ways,
In quiet nights that stretch like days.
A gentle touch, a knowing sigh,
Deep connections we can't deny.

From walls we build, we seek release,
In every bond, we find our peace.
Though miles apart, our souls entwine,
In shared moments, hearts align.

So let the cries for connection ring,
In every step, let love take wing.
For in this journey, hand in hand,
We forge a world, together we stand.

A Journey Within

Beneath the surface, whispers call,
A quest for truths, both great and small.
In quiet moments, shadows speak,
Revealing strength when we feel weak.

Through twisted paths of doubt and fear,
We stumble forth, our vision clear.
In every step, a lesson learned,
Through darkest nights, our spirits burned.

To understand the heart's deep maze,
We face our ghosts in silent gaze.
Each bitter tear, each joyful sigh,
A part of us that will not die.

As layers peel, new layers grow,
In every heart, a hidden glow.
With open minds, we shed our skin,
And find our peace, the journey within.

So take the time, explore your core,
In every moment, seek for more.
For within you lies the key,
To unlock doors, to truly be.

Embracing What Lies Beneath

In quiet depths where fears reside,
We ponder truths we often hide.
With gentle grace, we must explore,
The hidden parts we can't ignore.

For underneath the surface calm,
Lie roots of pain and fragile balm.
In shadows deep, the lessons wait,
To guide us past our self-made gate.

To feel, to hurt, to truly be,
Is to embrace our history.
With every scar, a testament,
To battles fought, to hearts unbent.

So dig the well, uncover bold,
The stories whispered, truths retold.
In acceptance, we find our strength,
In every moment, breadth and length.

With open arms and steady heart,
We learn to fear not being smart.
For in the depths where darkness lies,
Is where the brightest wisdom flies.

Gentle Waves of Affection

Softly they crest and fall,
Whispers of the heart's call,
Embracing in the moon's light,
Two souls dancing through the night.

Each wave tells a story true,
Carrying love just for you,
The ocean sings our refrain,
In every tide, joy and pain.

As dusk fades into deep blue,
Trust grows strong, a bond anew,
We ride the currents side by side,
On this vast, eternal tide.

Crashing shores and silent vows,
In gentle waves, our heart allows,
The ebb and flow of life's embrace,
Together we find our place.

In every dip and every rise,
Reflections dance in your eyes,
We surf the dreams we create,
In love's sweet waves, we elevate.

The Warmth of Understanding

In quiet moments shared so deep,
A bond that wraps like dreams in sleep,
Eyes meet in silent connection,
Creating warmth in every direction.

Holding hands through storms and sun,
Two hearts beat, becoming one,
A gentle touch, a knowing glance,
In understanding, we find our chance.

Words unspoken linger near,
In silence, hearts draw near,
Every laugh and every sigh,
We weave our story, you and I.

Through trials faced and shadows cast,
In the warmth, we hold steadfast,
Together we rise, we fall, we stand,
In this embrace, forever hand in hand.

With every challenge that we meet,
The warmth we share makes life sweet,
In understanding's gentle embrace,
We find our truth, our sacred space.

A Dance of Shared Sorrows

In the quiet corners of the night,
We find solace, hearts taking flight,
With every tear that falls in vain,
We dance together through the pain.

Shadows whisper, memories sting,
Yet we hold tight, the hope they bring,
Two souls twirl in muted grace,
In sorrow's arms, we find our place.

With each heartbeat, the music swells,
We share the stories darkness tells,
The weight we bear, we share as one,
In this dance, we have begun.

Through every ache and every sigh,
We pull each other, lift us high,
In the darkness, light is born,
In the midst of grief, love is sworn.

So let us twirl, let shadows sway,
In shared sorrows, we find our way,
Together we conquer, hearts entwined,
In this dance, our fate aligned.

Voices in the Abyss

Echoes linger in the dark,
Whispers of a flickering spark,
Calling softly to the lost,
In the abyss, we pay the cost.

The void sings a haunting song,
In its depths, we all belong,
Voices rise, entwined in fears,
Each one carrying silent tears.

Through shadows thick, we find the light,
Searching for solace in the night,
Together we wander, hand in hand,
Voices guiding across the land.

In the abyss, we share our plight,
Finding courage to ignite,
A flame that binds, a spark of grace,
In the darkness, we find our place.

So let the voices fill the air,
With every echo, show we care,
In the abyss, we find our way,
Together we'll face another day.

Fragments of Shared Stories

Whispers of laughter fill the air,
Memories woven with tender care.
In every glance, a tale unfolds,
Stories of warmth, like threads of gold.

Embers of past in our gentle gaze,
Moments that dance in a timeless haze.
The taste of joy in every bite,
Fragments that shine in the quiet night.

We gather close, our hearts combined,
In shared echoes, our souls aligned.
Each word a bridge, each sigh a song,
In these fragments, we all belong.

Pages turned, yet never erased,
In every story, love is interlaced.
Through laughter and tears, we carve our place,
In fragments of stories, we find our grace.

So let us share these tales anew,
In every heart, a spark breaks through.
For in these moments, we come alive,
In fragments of stories, we thrive.

Bonds Beyond Words

In silence we meet, where hearts collide,
A glance exchanged, where trust resides.
No need for speech, our spirits know,
The strength in bonds that gently grow.

Through laughter shared and tears unleashed,
In the tapestry of moments, we're released.
A thread unbroken, woven tight,
Together we rise, through day and night.

Each heartbeat echoes, a rhythm true,
In the embrace of friendship, we renew.
Beyond the words, our essence flows,
A language of love, that life bestows.

With every challenge, we stand our ground,
In unity's embrace, our strength is found.
Hand in hand, we weather the storm,
Bonds beyond words, forever warm.

Together we shine, like stars in the sky,
In every breath, together we fly.
The world may change, but we'll remain,
In bonds beyond words, we'll never wane.

The Pulse of Unity

In the heartbeat of the earth, we reside,
Connected through currents that gently guide.
We rise as one, in harmony's dance,
Each soul a note in this vibrant expanse.

In every stride, we share the weight,
In unity's rhythm, we celebrate fate.
As rivers flow, so do we blend,
A pulse of hope, our spirits mend.

Through trials faced, and joys amassed,
In every moment, shadows are cast.
But together we shine, lighting the way,
The pulse of unity, bright as day.

As voices rise in a gentle song,
Each note a promise, where we belong.
A tapestry bright, our lives entwined,
In the pulse of unity, hearts aligned.

With every heartbeat, our spirits soar,
Together we carry the hopes we store.
In the pulse of unity, we stand tall,
Connected forever, we'll never fall.

Journeying Through Another's Eyes

Step into my world, see what I see,
Each moment a doorway, a chance to be free.
Through the lens of my soul, let's wander wide,
In the tapestry of life, let's share the ride.

With every story, a lesson learned,
In the glow of kindness, a fire burned.
To walk in each other's shoes, we grow,
Journeying through paths we may not know.

Embrace the shadows, the light, and the dark,
For in every heartbeat, there lies a spark.
To understand depths, we must look within,
Journeying together, where love begins.

As we share our dreams, and fears laid bare,
In the quiet spaces, we find our care.
Through joy and sorrow, we'll find the way,
Journeying through another's eyes, we sway.

A world of colors, beyond the gray,
In the stories exchanged, we find our way.
Together we journey, hand in hand,
In the fabric of life, united we stand.

The Voice of Kindred Spirits

In quiet moments, we unite,
With whispered dreams in soft twilight.
Voices dance upon the breeze,
Echoing hearts, a gentle tease.

Through laughter shared, through tears that flow,
A bond unbroken, we both know.
Kindred spirits, drawn so near,
In every joy, in every fear.

Woven threads of fate entwined,
A tapestry of hearts aligned.
In this embrace, we find our song,
Together, we know we belong.

With every step, we walk side by side,
In this adventure, we take pride.
The voice of love, forever clear,
Guiding us through paths sincere.

So let us cherish this sacred light,
A beacon shining, warm and bright.
For in this world, we play our part,
Kindred spirits, heart to heart.

Ripples of Connection

A single stone can change the lake,
With gentle ripples, choices make.
Each act of courage, small yet grand,
Creates a wave across the land.

Connected hearts like branches sway,
In harmony through night and day.
Together we thrive, we rise, we fall,
Creating circles, a loving call.

In kindness shared, a spark ignites,
Illuminating darkest nights.
Each ripple spreads, embracing all,
Our hearts entwined, we will not stall.

With open arms, we gather near,
Through trials faced, through joy and fear.
A network strong, a bond so true,
Ripples of love, connecting through.

Let every whisper, every sigh,
Become a wave that lifts us high.
Together we'll weave a brighter fate,
In ripples of connection, we celebrate.

Shadows of a Caring Soul

In twilight's hush, where whispers dwell,
A caring heart weaves stories well.
Through shadows cast, compassion glows,
In gentle gestures, love bestows.

With every tear, a hand extends,
A soft embrace that never ends.
In silent moments, we find grace,
Shadows of kindness in every place.

Through trials faced, we learn to hold,
The warmth of empathy worth more than gold.
In every shadow, light reveals,
A caring soul, the heart that heals.

Together we'll walk, through dusk and dawn,
In every struggle, we are drawn.
Shadows linger, but love will soar,
Guiding us back to the heart's core.

So let us cherish, let us share,
In shadows found, a love laid bare.
For in each heart, a story lies,
A caring soul that never dies.

Waves of Kindness

From oceans deep, the waves arise,
With every crest, compassion flies.
A gentle surge of heartfelt grace,
Unites us all in this warm space.

In every smile, a ripple starts,
Flowing freely from loving hearts.
Together we ride, the highs and lows,
Through storms we face, our kindness grows.

With open hearts, we greet the tide,
In waves of kindness, hand in hand, we glide.
For in this journey, side by side,
We create a world where love won't hide.

Let kindness guide each step we take,
In every choice, the bonds we make.
For every wave, both big and small,
Will echo back, connecting us all.

So ride the waves, let kindness flow,
Embrace the journey, let love show.
With every breath, we'll find our way,
In waves of kindness, here we'll stay.

A Palette of Feelings

In every shade, emotions blend,
A brush of joy, a stroke of pain.
The canvas holds what words cannot,
In colors bright, hearts find their gain.

Hues of hope and deep despair,
Whispers soft in swirls of light.
Each stroke a journey, wild and rare,
A palette rich, a soul's delight.

Blues that crash like ocean waves,
Reds that pulse with love's embrace.
Yellows dance like sunlit saves,
In every hue, we find our place.

Greens of nature, calm and deep,
Purples shrouded in mystery.
Each color speaks, emotions seep,
A vibrant world, our history.

So let us paint with open hearts,
A masterpiece of all we feel.
In every art, a life departs,
A palette vast, our truths reveal.

The Hidden Symphony

In rustling leaves, the music plays,
A gentle breeze, a soft refrain.
The earth hums low in secret ways,
Nature's song, a sweet domain.

Birds take flight, their notes in air,
A symphony of life unfolds.
In every sound, love's whispered care,
A hidden world, its beauty holds.

Footsteps echo on the ground,
The heartbeat of the world we tread.
Echoes linger, love is found,
In silent notes, the heart is fed.

Waves collide in rhythmic dance,
As oceans chant their timeless tune.
Each moment sings, a fleeting glance,
Within the dark, we find the moon.

So pause and listen, take a breath,
To melodies that softly soar.
In every silence lies a depth,
The hidden symphony, ever more.

Weaving Threads of Trust

In gentle hands, the fibers spin,
Looms of faith in shadows cast.
Each thread a tale that we begin,
A tapestry of moments past.

Colors blend in soft embrace,
Golds of laughter, blues of tears.
In every stitch, we find our place,
A woven bond that calms our fears.

Embrace the fray, the knots of life,
For patterns shift with every turn.
Through joy and sorrow, love, and strife,
Together still, our hearts will yearn.

With every loop, we grow more bold,
Strength entwined in softest strands.
In stories shared, a warmth unfolds,
A canvas built by two kind hands.

So let us weave these threads of trust,
A fabric rich with honest grace.
In every knot, belief and rust,
A tapestry of love we trace.

Unspoken Bonds

In quiet moments, glances shared,
A world unseen, yet deeply felt.
No need for words, the heart has dared,
In silence, strong connections melt.

With every smile, a secret dance,
Fingers brush, the air is thick.
A life lived close, a fleeting chance,
In silent code, emotions click.

The touching warmth of knowing eyes,
A language framed in gentle looks.
In every heart, a wisdom lies,
With unspoken words, our story hooks.

Through trials faced, through laughter's glow,
The bond we share needs not be voiced.
Together through the ebb and flow,
In quiet strength, we find our choice.

So cherish these unseen, sweet threads,
The ties that hold, the love we gift.
In every glance that quietly spreads,
Unspoken bonds, a heartfelt lift.

Chords of Unseen Bonds

In shadows where our voices blend,
The heartbeat knows, our spirits mend.
Weaving threads through time and space,
In silent whispers, we find grace.

A smile shared, a gentle touch,
A glance that says so very much.
These quiet moments, soft and true,
Are chords that bind me close to you.

When storms may rise and skies grow dark,
Your laughter lights an inner spark.
Together we stand, hand in hand,
In unseen bonds, we understand.

Though miles may part our day-to-day,
In heart and soul, we find a way.
The music plays, through all we face,
A symphony of love and grace.

As seasons change and years unfold,
Our story's written, brave and bold.
Through each encounter, seed is sown,
Chords of unseen bonds have grown.

Songs of Silent Support

In quiet corners, hearts unite,
With every struggle, there's a light.
Support unfurls without a sound,
In songs of solace, hope is found.

A nod, a smile, a knowing glance,
Together we embrace each chance.
Through trials faced and dreams pursued,
In silent songs, our spirits brewed.

When whispers fade, and shadows creep,
Your strength awakens dreams from sleep.
With every word, every touch we share,
The bond we hold, beyond compare.

In laughter's echo, pain finds ease,
With you beside, my heart's at peace.
Through high and low, in joy and strife,
Your silent support brings me to life.

Together we rise, unfurling wings,
In harmony, our memory sings.
Through thick and thin, we rise, we soar,
In songs of support, forevermore.

Murmurs of Shared Journeys

On winding roads, our tales are spun,
Through every trial, battles won.
In murmurs soft, our secrets keep,
In shared journeys, dreams run deep.

With every step, the path unfolds,
New stories waiting to be told.
Through laughter's echo and teardrop's fall,
Together we rise, we stand tall.

As dusk descends and stars appear,
Your presence calms the stormy fear.
In whispered dreams beneath the skies,
Our hopes take flight, they rise, they rise.

Through days of sun and nights of grace,
In shared journeys, we find our place.
With every twist, with every turn,
In murmurs soft, our hearts discern.

And when our paths may fade from view,
The memories linger, strong and true.
In whispered tales of yesteryears,
Murmurs of us will dry the tears.

Footprints in Tenderness

In tender steps upon the earth,
Each footprint tells of love and worth.
With every stride, we leave a trace,
A gentle map of our embrace.

Through valleys deep and mountains high,
Together we dream, together we fly.
In light and shadow, hand in hand,
Footprints mark where we had planned.

As seasons shift and time moves on,
In every heart, a secret song.
With every journey, every glance,
In tenderness, we find our chance.

Across the sands, where memories blend,
Our footprints guide, despite the bend.
In every laugh, in every tear,
Tenderness grows, strong and clear.

And when we pause to look behind,
The path reveals what we may find.
In loving steps, forever free,
Footprints of love—the heart's decree.